ALL CHANGE!

**A Series of Six Teaching Sessions
Aimed at 5 - 7 year olds**

ACKNOWLEDGEMENTS

Material written and prepared by Eileen Booth, Diane Haley, Kath Langan,
  Pam Matheson, Christine Reid, Sue Stanworth and Elaine Williams.
'All Change' theme song by Penny Bainbridge
Artwork and design by Matthew Slater
Typesetting by Liz Potter
Additional help and advice from Tina Smith

Copyright © Crusaders 1993

First Published 1993
This edition printed by Crusaders 2000

ISBN 1 897987 03 X

All rights reserved. No part of this publication (other than the children's activity sheets for which specific permission is given) may be reproduced, stored in a retrieval system, or transmitted in any form or by any means, electronic, mechanical, photocopying, recording or otherwise, without the prior permission of Crusaders.

**Crusaders, 2 Romeland Hill, St Albans, Herts, AL3 4ET
01727 855422**
www.crusaders.org.uk
email@crusaders.org.uk

ALL CHANGE!

Contents

	All about 'All Change'.. ESSENTIAL information	2
Session 1	All Change at a Wedding Feast .... The Wedding at Cana (John 2:1-11)	5
Session 2	All Change for some Fishermen .... Jesus calls the First Disciples (Luke 5:1-11)	13
Session 3	All Change on a Stormy Sea .... Jesus Calms the Storm (Matthew 8:23-27)	21
Session 4	All Change for a Lonely Man .... Jesus and Zacchaeus (Luke 10:1-10)	29
Session 5	All Change for a Blind Man .... Jesus heals Bartimaeus (Mark 10:46-52)	41
Session 6	All Change for a Hungry Crowd .... Jesus feeds a crowd (Mark 6:30-44)	49
	The 'All Change' Theme Song	63
	The 'Things which were Changed by Jesus' Frieze.........	65

All About 'All Change!'

'All Change!' aims to introduce our 5 to 7 year olds to Jesus as the one who transformed the lives and circumstances of those He met. Simon, Zacchaeus, Bartimaeus (to mention just a few!) were never the same again after they had come face to face with the Son of God and seen for themselves His love and care, His unique power and how each of them were valued and special in His eyes.

Today, of course, we can still meet Jesus with the same life-changing consequences. 'All Change' focuses on six key incidents: in each session the children will be encouraged to find out something special about Jesus, think simply about how they can meet Him themselves and consider the changes He might bring to their lives!

All About Each Session

Activities designed to introduce the theme.

Set the Scene - a suggested 'lead-in' to the Bible Story.
Tell the Story - a suggested way of recounting the story, involving the children as much as possible.
(The story outlines is an embellishment of the Bible text, which you may want to change, adapt or ignore completely!)

The theme song (page 58) links the series.
The children learn a new verse each session and add it to the verses they have sung from previous stories.

The second link idea is a frieze, which is changed after each Bible story
to show the difference Jesus made (see Frieze supplement for detailed instructions).

A suggested procedure for helping children see the key points in each incident
and how to relate them simply to their own lives.

More activities, which develop or build on the theme.

It is most unlikely that you will be able to use the material just as you find it in this booklet!

We do suggest that you follow the

DO **HEAR** **SING** **SEE** **TALK, THINK AND PRAY** **DO**

pattern for each of your sessions, but you will also need to...

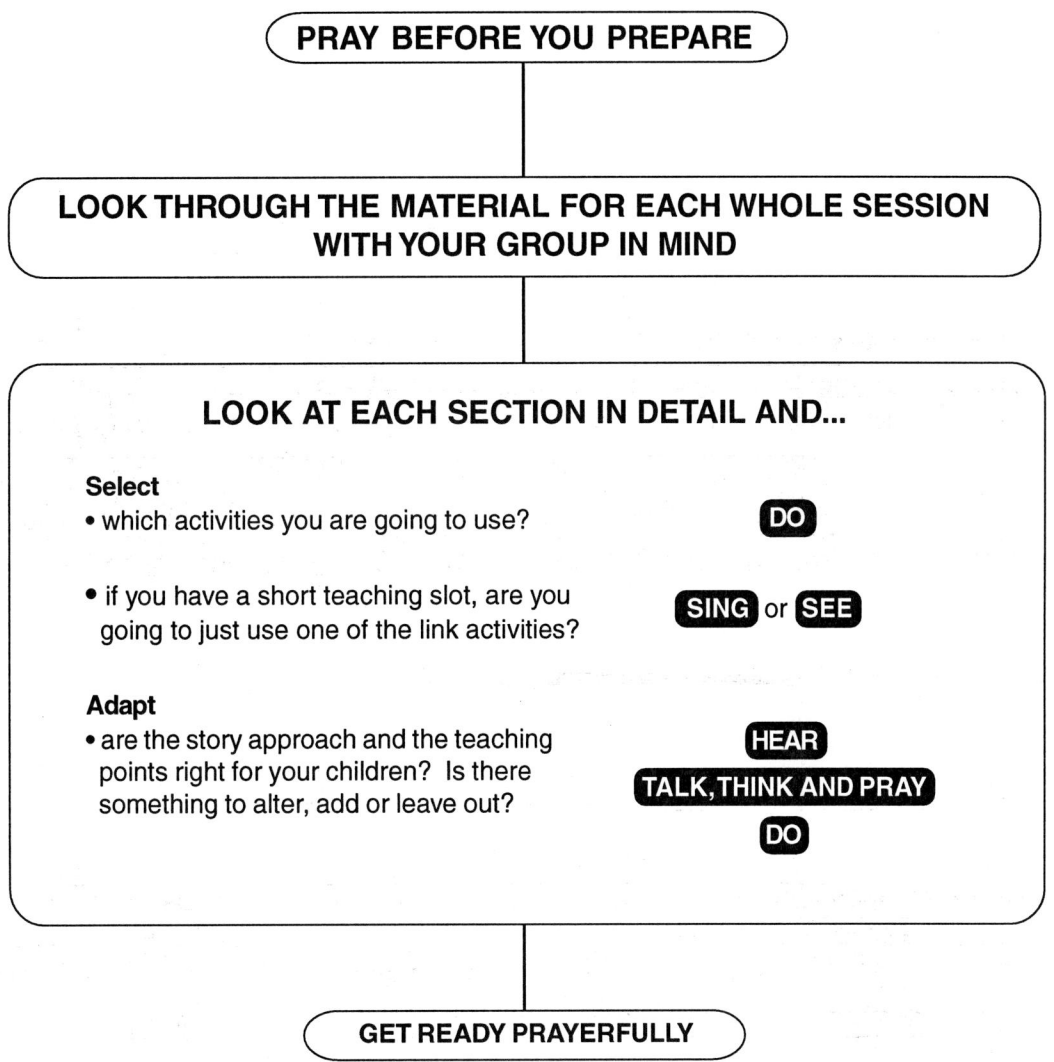

Just A Word About The Bible...

Children hear stories from many sources... it's absolutely essential that they understand the difference between these and the stories you will tell them from the Bible! You may need to build this into your programme, along the following lines:

- **right at the outset,** show a selection of books including the Bible - talk briefly about them all, but then say that the Bible is different and very special because God tells us very important things throughout it.

- **at the beginning of the HEAR section** each session, ask the children to remind you where the story comes from. Keep a Bible in front of you throughout, even if you are not reading directly from it!

There are several good Bibles for children available now (paraphrasing the original text) - Among the best are:

The Beginner's Bible (Kingsway)   **The Children's Bible in 365 Stories** (Lion)
The Lion Children's Bible (Lion)   **The Ladybird Bible Story Book** (Ladybird)

Finally... and most importantly, let's pray that the children in our groups will meet Jesus for themselves and be ready and willing for Him to bring change into their lives!

These symbols are used throughout 'All Change!':

☆   **A point to make or something to say**

▶   **To do in advance**

➡   **An instruction to you as leader**

Session 1
ALL CHANGE AT A WEDDING FEAST
John 2:1-11

> WE WANT THE CHILDREN ... to see that Jesus is really special.

This is a good opportunity to have a small party, perhaps to launch a new group or just to start this series.

YOU WILL NEED
To send out the invitations

- Send out invitations before your meeting - a sample invitation to photocopy is provided on page 11).

Party food
Decorations

- Set the scene for a party: lay out tables with drinks and simple party food, such as crisps and biscuits, before the children arrive - decorate the room with balloons and streamers if you wish!

1. **Party Games**
   Play one or two simple party games, such as:

YOU WILL NEED
To prepare a parcel!
Music
A bag of wrapped sweets

- - *Pass the parcel*

  - *Musical statues* or *Musical bumps*

  - *Hide the sweet* (one child leaves the room whilst a sweet is hidden somewhere around the room - when the child returns, the other children shout 'cold', 'warm', 'hot' and so on, according to how close the child is to the hidden sweet! Sweets which are found may, of course, be eaten!)

2. **Buttonholes**
   Choose one of these two ways, **A** or **B**, to make paper flower buttonholes, such as a wedding guest might wear!

YOU WILL NEED
Card, scissors, glue, stapler, sellotape, safety pins, different coloured tissue paper.
To prepare card shapes

- **A.** In advance, cut out simple flower shapes from card - each flower should measure about 6 cm across.

  1. Give a flower shape to each child.

  2. Let the children tear off small pieces of coloured tissue, scrunch them up, and stick them all over their flower shape.

  3. Sellotape a safety pin to the back of the buttonhole - and put it on!

7

> B. In advance, cut out card circles (enough for one per child) and tissue circles (enough for three or four per child) - all circles should measure about 6cm across. Use pinking shears if you have them!

    1. Give a card circle to each child.

    2. Ask each child to choose three or four coloured tissue circles.

    3. Place the tissue circles on top of the card and staple them together in the middle.

    4. Pull the tissue circles forward and scrunch them gently to form a 3-D flower.

    5. Sellotape the safety pin to the back of the buttonhole - and wear it!

✚ Ask the children to imagine that they are going to a wedding and invite them to choose something special to wear from a dressing-up box.

◄ **YOU WILL NEED**
To prepare Card shapes

◄ **YOU MAY NEED**
Dressing-up clothes

HEAR

Set the Scene...

➡ Invite the children to sit down around the tables.

➡ Pour the drinks and share out some of the food.

➡ As the children are finishing, ask for quiet and begin the story...

Tell the story twice -

THE FIRST TIME, simply read it, perhaps with other leaders playing some of the key roles.

THE SECOND TIME, have the children take part:

> In advance, write out **Jesus, Mary, the bride, the groom** and **the man in charge** on separate slips of paper - write **a servant** and **a wedding guest** on a number of other slips of paper. Fold them together individually and put them in a container.

➡ Let the children each take one of the pieces of paper, and ask them to mime the actions of that person as you read the story...

◄ **YOU WILL NEED**
To prepare slips of paper
A pot or container

Story

Jesus and Mary, His mum, were once invited to a very special party - it was a wedding feast in a town called Cana, a little way from where they lived. The bride and groom were there, of course, and many of their friends and relations had come as guests. There were lots of delicious things to eat and drink. There was music and dancing. Everyone was talking and laughing and having a really good time. But then Mary noticed the worried looks on the faces of some of the servants: she listened carefully to what they were whispering to each other...

"There's no more wine left!"
"Oh no!"
"It's completely run out: my master will be very upset!"
"Whoever heard of a wedding with no wine! What are we going to do?"

Mary told Jesus what had happened, and then she said to the servants:

"Do whatever Jesus tells you to"

Nearby stood six huge jars made of stone. Jesus said:

"Fill these jars with water"

So the servants ran and fetched water and filled all the jars right to the top.

"Now pour some out and take it to the man in charge"

said Jesus. The servants looked at each other - what would the man in charge say when they poured plain old water into his cup? But they did what Jesus said. As they poured, they could hardly believe their eyes - Jesus had changed the water into wine! The man in charge tasted it.

"Mmmm! This is delicious!" he said. Then he turned to the bridegroom,

"at every wedding the best wine is served first of all, but you have saved the most delicious wine 'til last!"

And so the wedding feast could go on...

The chorus and first verse of the 'All Change!' theme song
- see page 58.

SEE

Complete part one of the frieze: 'fill' the empty jars by:
- colouring
- painting
- sticking on material or coloured paper.

YOU WILL NEED
The frieze (see Supplement)
Pens
Paints or material and glue

TALK, THINK AND PRAY

★ Ask: *What have you found out about Jesus?*

★ Bring out particularly Jesus' special powers and how only He was able to make the wedding problem turn out right.

★ Mention that Jesus was very pleased to be invited to the wedding.

★ Go on to say that Jesus would like us to invite Him into all our situations - into the happy times and into the sad ones!

★ Emphasise this by explaining that Jesus wants to change things for the better for us too... we only have to invite Him!

★ **PRAY**
   ... asking the children to suggest specific 'happy times' and thank God for them.

   ... thanking Jesus that He is really special and that He can change things for the better.

   ... inviting Him into the happy times and into the sad times.

1. Photos
Following the wedding theme, ask the children to pose for small and large group photos. Have these developed and display them as soon as possible!

YOU WILL NEED
A loaded camera

2. Invitations
➤ In advance, make photocopies of the outline on page 11 - enough for one per child.

★ Say that we can invite our friends to find out how special Jesus is by asking them to come to our group.

Let the children colour the invitations and write in their friend's name and the details appropriate to your group. Encourage them to give out the invitations before the next session!

YOU WILL NEED
To make photo-copies of the invitation
Coloured pens, pencils or crayons.

3. Decorating Biscuits
Ask the children to decorate a plain biscuit, using blobs of coloured icing and scattering currants, 'hundreds and thousands' or chocolate buttons. Put them out to eat as you continue the party...

YOU WILL NEED
Plain biscuits
Bowls of different coloured icing
Simple decorations
Spoons

4. Take home cake
Following usual party traditions, at the end of the session, cut a cake (something simple, such as a swiss roll would be fine) or have individual cakes for the children to take home.

YOU WILL NEED
A cake or individual cakes
Kitchen paper roll

Crusader Special

_____ is invited to a

Crusader Special

on _____ from _____ to _____

place _____

See you there!

Crusaders

Dear _____

Please come to

Crusaders

on _____ days

from _____ to _____

at _____

_____

P.S. Parents, please ring _____ for more information.

Session 2
ALL CHANGE FOR SOME FISHERMEN
Luke 5:1-11

> **WE WANT THE CHILDREN...** to see how Jesus chooses ordinary people and gives them a special job to do.

YOU WILL NEED
To prepare a
job basket

1. **Job basket**
   - In advance, write out on separate pieces of paper jobs which need doing at some time during your session - for example:
     put out the cups
     help make the drinks
     hand out the pencils
     say 'hello' to anybody new... and so on.
   You will need one 'job' for each child. Fold the papers individually and put them in a small basket or container.

   1. As the children arrive for the session, ask them to take a piece of paper from the 'job basket'.

   2. Explain that this is their special job to do at some time before they go home.

   3. Remember to comment and to thank each child as he/she completes his/her task!

YOU WILL NEED
To set up the room

2. **Choose your boat**
   - In advance, put out two sets of chairs, or two mats to represent two boats.

   1. Ask the children to imagine that they are outside in the fresh air by the sea.... (add a detailed description if you wish!) - establish the chairs or mats as boats, and explain that one belongs to SIMON and the other to JAMES and JOHN.

   2. Ask two leaders to stand face to face to hold hands and then to lift their hands up high to form an arch.

   3. Ask the children to make a line and to run through the arch and round and round.

   4. Begin to sing, to the tune of 'London Bridge is falling down':
      "both the boats are leaving now, leaving now,
      *   leaving now*
      both the boats are leaving now
      choose yours quickly!"

13

5. As you sing the last line, the leaders pull down their arms to catch one child - he/she must choose either 'SIMON'S BOAT' or 'JAMES and JOHN'S BOAT' and then goes to sit down.

6. Continue until all the children have sat down in one of the two boats!

HEAR

Ask one leader to sit in each of the 'boats' as 'captain': as you tell the story, ask the leaders to mime the suggested actions, and the children to listen carefully and copy what their 'captain' is doing!

Story

Simon was very tired (action - yawning, stretching, sighing). He had been out all night fishing (action - throwing nets over ships) but had not caught one single fish (action - shaking heads) and it was now morning as he and his friends rowed to shore (action - rowing). They got out of their boats and began washing their nets (action - getting out and washing nets). As they were doing this, a crowd of people began to arrive on the shore to listen to Jesus who was telling them all about God's love. Simon's boat was near by and as he washed his nets he listened to what Jesus had to say (action - listening - by cupping hand on ear).

Soon there were so many people on the shore that there was no more room for Jesus, so He walked towards Simon's boat and got in. He told Simon and his friends to row a little way out (action - getting in and rowing), then Jesus told Simon to stop rowing (action - stop!) and began to talk to the people again. All the time Jesus was talking, Simon listened (action - listening). When Jesus finished talking to the people and they began to leave, He said to Simon:

"Row out into deeper water and throw out your nets to catch fish" (action -Simon's Boat - rowing).
Simon said to Jesus

"We've been out fishing all night and haven't caught anything, but we'll try again, Jesus, because you have told us to" (action - throwing nets over boat).

As they pulled in their nets they could feel there were lots and lots of fish in them, so they pulled harder and harder on the nets (action - Simon's boat - pulling heavy nets up). Soon they could feel the nets beginning to break, and so they called over to their friends in the other boat to help them (action - Simon's boat - waving arms and beckoning to other boat - both boats pull hard on nets). There were so many fish in the nets that soon both boats began to sink. Simon realised how special

Jesus was and he said to Jesus "I'm not good enough to be with you Jesus, please go away", but Jesus looked at him and said "Don't be frightened Simon, I've got a special job I want you to do. You won't be catching fish anymore, I want you to come and work with me".

Jesus chose Simon and his friends, ordinary fishermen, to go and tell people just how much God loves them. So Simon and his friends got out of their boats (action - getting out), pulled their boats on to the shore (action - pulling boats up), left their boats and followed Jesus (action - following for a short distance).

SING

The first two verses of the 'All Change' theme song - see page 58.

SEE

YOU WILL NEED
To prepare the figure
Frieze
Blu-tack

➤ In advance, copy, colour and cut out the figure.

➡ Tack it next to the figure on the second part of the frieze...

TALK, THINK AND PRAY

★ Ask the children to look at the two figures on the frieze: **What is different about the two pictures?** (You may need to make it clear that they both represent one of the fishermen!).

★ Now ask: **Can you think what has happened to make the fisherman happy?**

★ Emphasise particularly that Jesus chose Simon, James, John and other friends and gave them a special and important job to do.

★ State that everyone is special to Jesus and that He still asks people today to work with Him to help others.

★ Ask: **Can you think of any special jobs you could do to help Jesus and help others?** (for example, helping out at home, being kind, sharing sweets... and so on)

★ **PRAY**
... thanking God for people who help us

... thanking Jesus that we are all special to Him

... asking God to show us how we can help others.

1. Team Challenge

Building on the theme that we are all different but equally special, set up a series of challenges, which should involve all the members of a small team.

A. <u>Establishing the Team</u>

1. Divide the children into teams of 5 or 6 (no more than 6).

2. Ask each team to:
   - choose a team name.
   - use the paper to draw a 'team emblem', which can be sellotaped down one side to the stick or cane to make a flag - the picture might be linked with the team name.
   - choose a team captain.

3. The captain of each team in turn should walk around the room carrying the team's flag, with the rest of the team walking behind - all the other children should applaud!

B. <u>Set the Challenges</u>

For each of the following five challenges:
- explain what is involved
    - let each team choose one of its team
members
    - do the challenge
    - award points as appropriate

(NB - Do make sure that nobody is left out, perhaps by limiting the number of times each child can take part)

1. HOPPING - see who can hop on one leg for the longest time... children are 'out' when they put the other foot down on the floor!

2. QUIZ - ask the 'contestants' to answer three general knowledge questions - award a point for each correct answer:
   ● What is Everest? (World's highest mountain)
   ● What does BFG stand for? (Big Friendly Giant)
   ● What colour is a panther? (Black)

3. JIGSAW - time the children one-by-one to see who can complete the jigsaw in the quickest time (NB - don't let them watch each other!)

4. STRING HOOP - standing the contestants in a line with their arms stretched up in the air, put the string hoop over them one-by-one and award a point to each child who can wiggle through the hoop until it falls to the floor!

5. RELAY RACE - let each team choose three quick runners to go one after the other in a mini relay race - the quickest trio wins a point for their team.

YOU WILL NEED
Plain paper
A stick, cane (or ruler) for each group
Coloured pens, pencils or crayons
Sellotape

YOU WILL NEED
Paper and pens

YOU WILL NEED
To make a simple jigsaw by cutting a piece of card into interesting shapes
A stopwatch

YOU WILL NEED
A length of string or cord 65 cm long, tied to form a hoop

✭ Do try to bring out the fact that the different people in the team were needed for the different challenges.

2. How Can I Help?

Developing the idea that Jesus calls us to work with Him to help others, talk with the children about the two situations in turn:

What can you see in the picture?
Is there anything wrong at all?
How could you help if you were there?

Ask the children to:

1. Draw themselves helping out in some way in each picture.

2. Colour the pictures in to take home.

YOU WILL NEED ➤
To make photocopies of the park and home pictures on pages 18 and 19.
Coloured pen, pencils or crayons

3. People Who Help Us - display poster

➤ In advance, paint or write in bold pens on the large piece of coloured paper: **Thank you, Jesus, for people who help us.**

➥ 1. Ask the children to think of a person who especially helps them - this could be general (eg a doctor) or specific (eg a parent or particular friend).

2. Each child should then draw and paint the person.

3. The pictures can be cut out and stuck to the coloured paper to make a poster to display.

NEXT SESSION: the children will be dressing up for stormy weather... ask them <u>now</u> to bring something suitable to wear!

YOU WILL NEED ➤
To prepare one large piece of coloured paper
Paper
Coloured pens, pencils, crayons or paints
Pencils
Scissors
Glue

Session 3
ALL CHANGE ON A STORMY SEA
Matthew 8:23-27

> **WE WANT THE CHILDREN...** to appreciate more of Jesus' special powers and to trust that He will help us face the things which frighten us.

REMEMBER: you asked the children to bring wet weather gear? Some will have forgotten, so have some spares!

1. Bubbles

YOU WILL NEED
To make tubs of bubbles (or buy them!)

➤ In advance, buy bubble tubs **OR** make up a fairly concentrated mix of washing-up liquid and water in a container - twist pipe-cleaners to make 'blowers'!

✯ Talk about the wind - what it feels like, how it can sometimes be soft and sometimes be strong. What it does (eg blowing leaves off the trees in autumn; providing power to move yachts and sailing boats and windmills.)

Now see who's good at blowing! Let the children blow bubbles from tubs you have bought or from your home-made mixture.

2. Bad Weather - get ready!

YOU WILL NEED
A die
One set of adult bad weather gear (raincoat, wellies, hat... and so on)
Small sweets, fruit or nuts as prizes

1. Sit all the children in the circle and put the clothes in a pile in the middle.

2. Explain that the number six on the die represents stormy weather and so anyone who throws a six needs to put on all the clothes they see in the middle of the circle.

3. Start to pass the die around with each child taking a turn to throw it. If a child who throws a six manages to put everything on, he/she is awarded a mini prize **but** the other children go on passing round the die, and anyone who gets a six takes over in the centre.

Set the Scene...

➡ Bring the children together as a whole group and talk about the weather, along the following lines:
  What kinds of weather do you like best?
  Can the weather sometimes be frightening? (mention thunderstorms and strong winds - the children might also have heard about hurricanes or floods in other countries)

21

★ Go on to talk about the weather today... say you don't like it much and ask the children to help you change it by shouting at it - for example, *"it's raining now, so let's shout at the rain and make it stop"* - establish that we cannot do this, but that somebody in our story can!

★ Get the children dressed up in their raincoats and wellies ready to take part in the story.

➤ **Tell the story -**

➡ Divide your group in half - one half will play Jesus' friends (JF) and the other half will be the storm (S).

➡ Allocate a leader to each half.

➡ Ask the leaders to quickly rehearse the actions, sound and words for the story (without saying what actually happens in the end).

➡ Tell it TWICE, swapping the children round so that everybody plays both the storm and one of Jesus' friends.

◄ **YOU WILL NEED**
To brief two leaders

YOU MAY NEED
Simple percussion instruments to sound like rain and thunder

Story

Jesus got into a boat with his friends **(action JF - sit on the floor as if in a boat)**. Jesus was very tired and He fell asleep. Jesus' friends set off from the shore and started to sail across the lake. All was calm and the boat rocked gently from side to side **(action JF - sway)**. Then the wind began to blow harder and harder **(action JF - move faster from side to side; action S - blow and make 'whooshing' sound like the wind and waves)** It started to rain hard **(action S - tap with one finger on the palm of the other hand or use a tambourine)**. The lightning flashed and it began to thunder **(action S - clap or bang on a drum)**. The boat bobbed high up in the waves and then bobbed down in the water **(action JF - move accordingly)**. Everyone in the boat was very frightened **(action JF - shout out things like "I'm frightened!" "I'm scared!!""What is going to happen to us?")**. Jesus' friends woke Him up **(action JF - shout "wake up, Jesus!2 + leader - shout "Jesus, please help us or we're all going to drown!")**. Jesus stood up and told the wind and the rain and the thunder and the lightning to stop... and there was complete peace and quiet **(action EVERYBODY - be totally silent)**. All Jesus' friends were amazed because even the wind and the waves on the sea did what He said.

SING

The first three verses of the 'All Change' theme song (see page 58).

SEE

YOU WILL NEED
To prepare the calm waters
The frieze
Blu-tack

➤ In advance, colour the calm water blue and cut along the line of the waves.

➡ On the third part of the frieze, show the boat bobbing up and down on the stormy sea. Stick the calm blue waters on, and show the boat set straight, just swaying gently.

TALK, THINK, AND PRAY

✯ Ask: **How did Jesus' friends feel when the storm was really bad?**

✯ Say that there are things which frighten us - mention, if appropriate, examples or things which you are afraid of.

✯ Ask: **What sort of things can make us afraid?** - Do be very sensitive and control the situation so that fear is not spread.

✯ State, very clearly and confidently, that Jesus is with us all the time and that He is stronger than anything or anybody who scares us.

✯ Go on to say that He can help us not to be frightened any more if we ask Him to.

✯ **PRAY**

... thanking God for the different kinds of weather
... thanking God for Jesus, who is with us all the time
... asking for help with those things which scare us
... specifically for individual children and their needs.

DO

YOU WILL NEED
Mats
A small prize

1. **Shipwreck!**
    1. Scatter mats around the room, and explain that they represent lifeboats!

    2. Ask the children to move round, not touching the 'lifeboats' at all and say <u>how</u> they should move (walk, run, hop, skip, or crawl...).

    3. When you shout 'shipwreck', the children must get on to a 'lifeboat' - the last one on a mat is out!

23

4. Choose a different way of moving round after each 'shipwreck'.

5. Award a small prize to the winner - the last child left in the game.

2. Paper Boats

Make paper boats - see page 25 for instructions. Try them out in a bowl of water to see if they will float! If you have space, organise boat races between children who can blow their boats along.

YOU WILL NEED
Plain paper (A4 size)
Coloured pens, crayons or paints
Sellotape
A bowl of water

3. Weather Calendars

Following the weather theme, let the children colour and decorate their own weather calendar - draw attention to the verse on the bottom. Ask the children to take them home and fill in daily a picture to show what the weather has been like. (You could organise a mini-competition if you wish, awarding prizes to children who bring a completed calendar to the next session.)

YOU WILL NEED
To make photocopies of page 26, enough for one per child
Coloured pens or pencils

HOW TO MAKE A PAPER BOAT

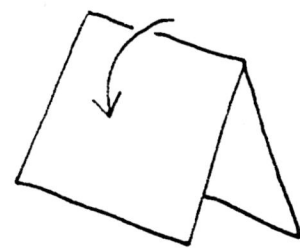

1. Fold an A4 piece of paper in half.

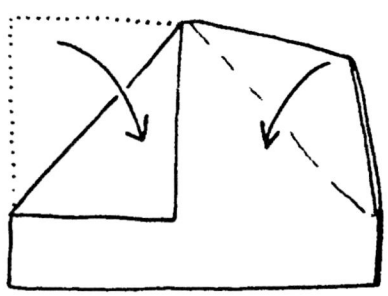

2. Fold the top corners inwards so they meet in the middle.

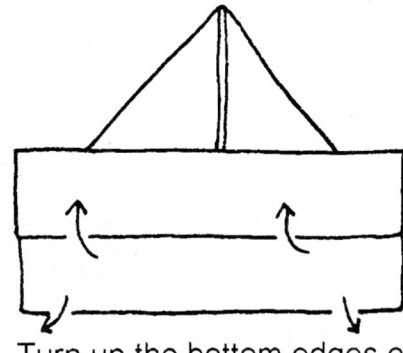

3. Turn up the bottom edges on one side, turn over and repeat on the other side.

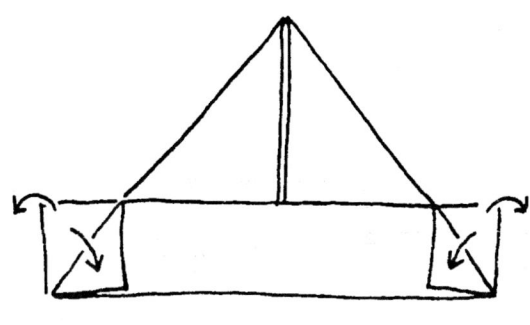

4. Fold down the corners as shown on each side and stick them down with tape or glue.

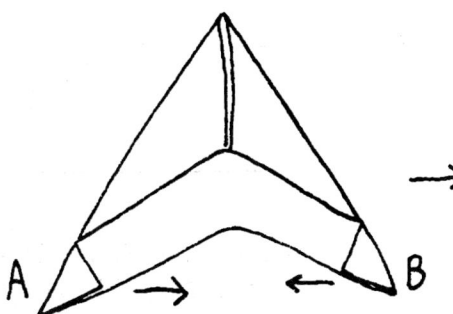 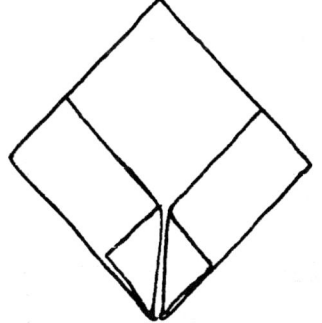

5. Push the two ends A and B together so that a square is formed.

6. Fold the bottom half up on one side, turn over and repeat on the other side. Then push the two ends C and D together to make another square.

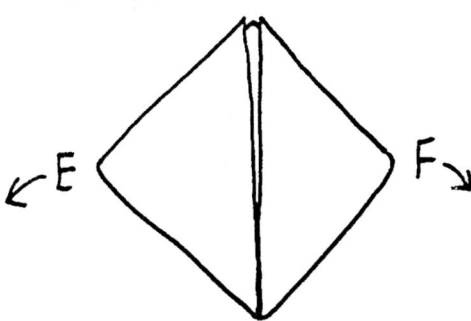

7. Pull the two sides E and F firmly apart to form the boat and open up the bottom so that it will stand up.

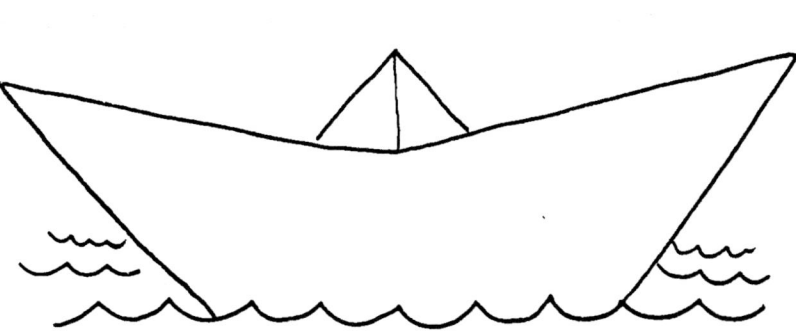

25

Session 4
ALL CHANGE FOR A LONELY MAN
Luke 19:1-10

> **WE WANT THE CHILDREN...** to understand that Jesus loves everybody, even those whom nobody else loves, and that He asks us to love other people too! To know that He forgives us and helps us put things right.

YOU WILL NEED
A small prize

1. **Clumps**

    1. Ask the children to move around the room.

    2. After a minute or so, call out any number from '2' to '8'.

    3. If you shout '3', for example, the children must get into a group of 3, hold hands and sit down together to form a 'clump'.

    4. Any child/children left over are 'out'.

    5. Continue the game, varying the number you call out, until you have a winner.

2. **This is a really good game...!**

YOU WILL NEED
To brief two leaders in advance
6 x anything, as long as they are all the same 1 x a different object

➤ Prepare this carefully in advance! The leaders playing the game need to understand the 'secret' so that it runs smoothly.

➡ 1. Ask the two leaders to sit opposite each other, and sit the children down so that they can all see what is happening.

2. Say what a good game this is - really go overboard on this!

3. Explain that the two leaders will start and that everybody else can join in as soon as they catch on...

4. The first leader throws the 7 objects on the floor - the other leader looks at them <u>hard</u>. At the same time, the first leader rests a number of fingers on his/her knee - this is the signal! The second leader notes how many fingers are there, and says this number <u>only</u>. The first leader congratulates the second leader, and hands over the objects for the second leader's turn.

27

5. The game goes on, with the leaders taking it in turn to throw the objects.

6. After 2 or 3 rounds, ask the children (and other leaders) to join in. They will, of course, think it has something to do with the objects and come up with all sorts of possibilities - it is most unlikely that anybody will catch on.

HEAR

Set the Scene...

★ Ask about either of the games: *How did it feel to be left out?*

★ Talk briefly about other situations in which the children might be left out (eg games, friendship groups) emphasising how it feels each time.

➡ Hand out 4 sweets or nuts to each child.

➤ As you do this, have another leader move noisily around the group collecting back two sweets or nuts from each child and saying things like *"Give me some of those for the leaders!"*, (aside - *"I'll keep some of them for myself!"*).

➡ When sweets or nuts have been taken from everybody the leader should hand one or two over to his/her co-leaders, but make it very obvious that he/she is keeping most for him/herself.

★ Ask: *What do you think about this?*

➡ Have the leader munch his/her way quietly through the sweets or nuts as you tell the story...

Tell the story

Story

This story is about a man called Zacchaeus, who lived in Jericho. His job was collecting money from people to help build new roads and hospitals and all the other things needed in a city. All the same, people did not like paying this money - even today, grown-ups grumble about giving away money out of their wages, but it's a good idea because it pays for the important things we need in our towns! Anyway, people did not like Zacchaeus at all, because, a bit like ..... **(name of leader who collected back sweets, nuts)**, he took more money than was really needed and kept some for himself. He became very rich... but he was very lonely because nobody liked him and he had not got any friends.

One day, on his way home from work, Zacchaeus saw crowds of people who had all come to see Jesus. He decided that he would like to see Jesus too. He had heard that Jesus was a very special man. Zacchaeus could not see, because he was a very

YOU WILL NEED
To brief a leader in advance
A packet of small sweets or nuts

Q. Do your parents ever say they haven't got enough money.

Q. Do you like going to a friends house for tea / having a friend for tea.

Q. Have you ever been at the back of a crowd & can't see?

little man. He tried standing on tiptoes, but he still could not see. He tried to push his way through the crowd, but when people saw who he was, they would not let him through. Then he had an idea: he saw a sycamore tree growing nearby - he could climb the tree, sit in the branches and be able to see everything! And so he did.

After a little while, Zacchaeus could see Jesus coming along the road with His friends. When Jesus got to the tree, He stopped and looked stright up into the branches, where Zacchaeus was sitting.

"Come down, Zacchaeus!", Jesus said "I would like to come home to tea with you today!". Zacchaeus was really surprised...

★ Ask: **Why do you think Zacchaeus was so surprised?**
(Jesus knew His name; Jesus wanted to come to tea with him - nobody else would!)

...and he quickly climbed down the tree and went home to prepare a meal for his important visitor.

Jesus had tea with Zacchaeus. After they had eaten, Jesus said that He knew how wrongly Zacchaeus was behaving. Zacchaeus felt ashamed: he knew he had been wrong to live as he did while the people who lived near him were poor and hungry. He knew that he had been selfish and very greedy. He decided straightaway to make up for all the bad things he had done by giving poor people half of everything he had. He also paid all the people the extra money he had taken for himself.

➡ Have the leader give three sweets or nuts to each child.

YOU WILL NEED
Another packet of sweets or nuts!

When he had done all this, Zacchaeus felt really good inside. He felt happier than he had ever done before!

SING

The first four verses of the 'All Change!' theme song - see page 58.

SEE

YOU WILL NEED
To prepare the figures
The frieze
Glue

➤ In advance, copy, colour and cut out the faces.

➡ Add them to Zacchaeus' house, as he is no longer a sad and lonely man!

TALK, THINK AND PRAY

* Ask:
  - *What was Zacchaeus like <u>before</u> he met Jesus?*
  - *What was Zacchaeus like <u>after</u> he met Jesus?*
  - *Why do you think Zacchaeus was so happy at the end of the story?*

* Bring out especially that:
  - Zacchaeus realised just how much Jesus loved him.
  - Zacchaeus felt better because he had put right the wrong things he had done.

* Say that this can make us very happy too, because Jesus...
  - loves each one of us very much;
  - can forgive us for the things we sometimes do wrong, (ask for suggestions) and help

* **PRAY**
  ... thanking Jesus that He loves us so much.
  ... saying 'sorry' for the selfish and hurtful things we do sometimes.
  ... asking for His help to put them right.

DO

1. Puzzle Sheet
To reinforce the message of the meeting between Jesus and Zacchaeus, let the children work through and colour in a copy of the puzzle sheet on page 32.

YOU WILL NEED
In advance photocopy the puzzle sheet on page 32.

2. 'Thank you' Flower Card
* Introduce this by saying that Jesus loves everyone, and that He asks us to love other people too.

* Ask the children to just think of the people (and maybe also the animals!) they love.

* Go on to say how nice it is to show these special people that we love them...

➡ Make 'thank you' flower cards - see instructions on page 34. Encourage the children to take them home and give them out.

YOU WILL NEED
Coloured paper
Scissors
Coloured pens and pencils
Glue or sellotape

3. Sweets to give away
* Again, state that Jesus loves us and asks us to love others too!

* Say, again, that it's good to show people that we care for them...

Make some sweets - see instructions page 36.

YOU WILL NEED
The appropriate ingredients (recipes p.36)
Sweet papers
A large mixing bowl
Large & small spoons...

[Make it clear that these are to take home and give away! Alternatively, take the sweets to an old people's home, or to someone the children might know who is unwell...]

With this age group, you will be able to make the sweets altogether, with individual children adding separate ingredients, stirring the mixture and so on.

JESUS MEETS ZACCHAEUS

Can you find 10 differences between these two pictures?
Circle them in the picture on the right.

NOW can you complete the message?

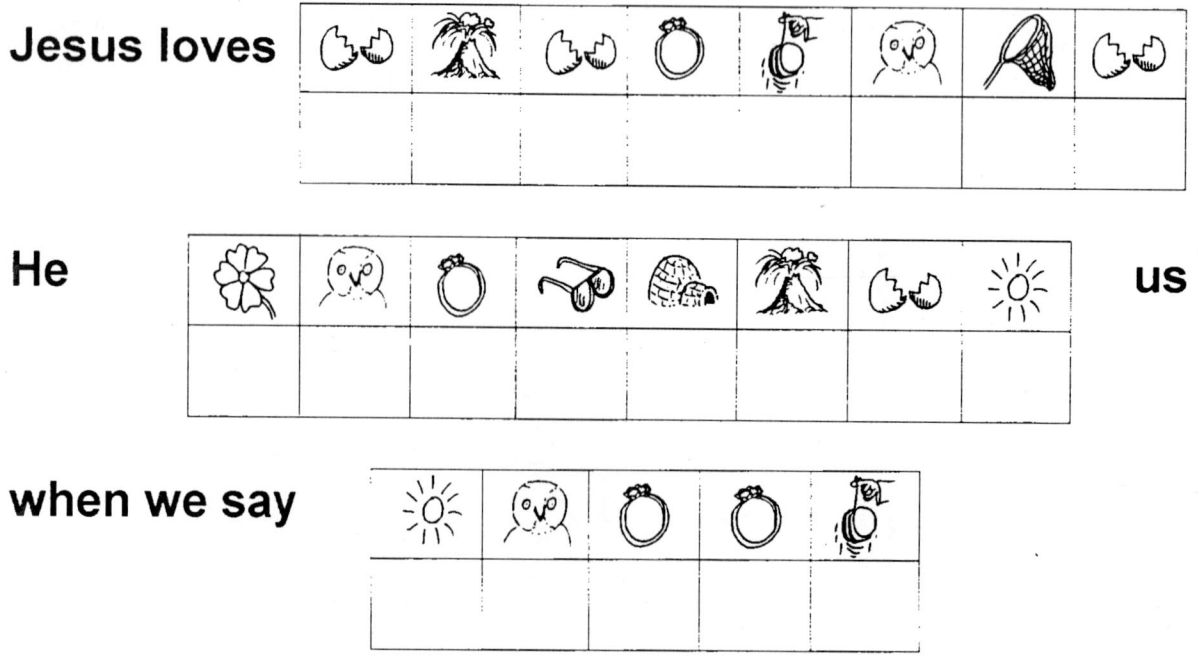

JESUS MEETS ZACCHAEUS

Can you find 10 differences between these two pictures?
Circle them in the picture on the right.

NOW can you complete the message?

Jesus loves e v e r y o n e

He f o r g i v e s **us**

when we say s o r r y

HOW TO MAKE 'THANK YOU' FLOWER CARDS

➡ In advance, prepare the coloured paper. For each 'card' you will need:

1 square of coloured paper, measuring 20 cm x 20 cm.
1 square of a different coloured paper, measuring 12 cm x 12 cm.

➡ Make the flower shape from the largest square of paper

1. Fold the paper in half, then in half again and then in half again!

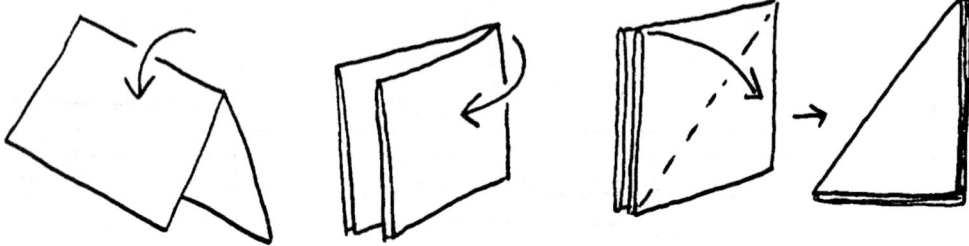

2. Cut a scallop shape into the paper.

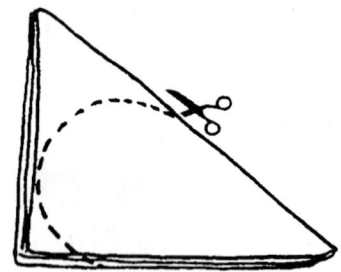

3. Open out the flower shape, and write a 'thank you' message inside.

4. Fold the flower back together again.

➡ Make the envelope from the smaller square of paper:

1. Fold one corner into the centre of the square, then fold the sides in and stick one on top of the other as shown.

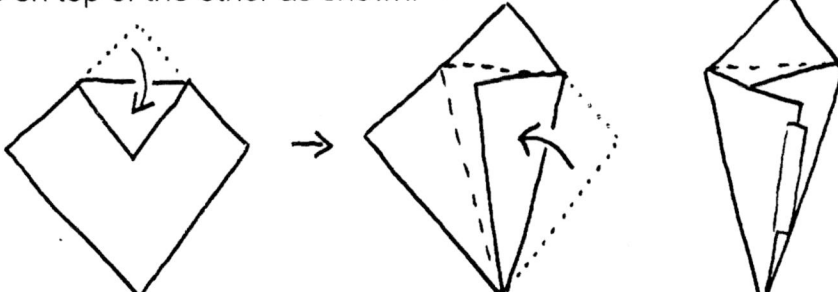

2. Now pop the flower inside, and either stick down or tuck in the top flap.

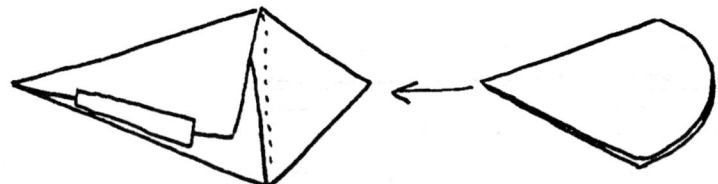

3. Write the person's name on the outside... and pass the card on!

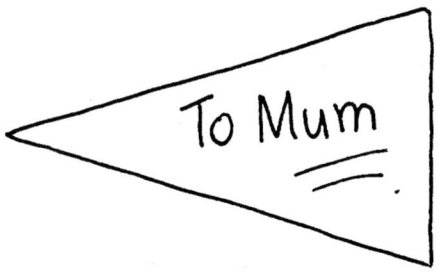

Adapted from an idea by Lois Rock in the *Simply Wonderful Craftbook* (Lion). Used with permission.

SWEET RECIPES

Rosehip Dreams

225g/8oz sieved icing sugar
1 tablespoon rosehip syrup
1 tablespoon lemon juice
Finely grated rind of 1/2 lemon
20 crystallised flowers to decorate

Method: Mix the icing sugar, rosehip syrup, lemon juice and rind to a stiff paste. Roll into 20 balls on a work surface liberally sprinkled with icing sugar.

Press a crystallised flower on each and place in sweet paper. Chill.

Makes 20 sweets.

Peanut Butter Creams

40g/1 1/2oz full fat soft cheese
200g/7oz sieved icing sugar
2 tablespoons peanut butter
2-3 drops vanilla essence
25g/1oz salted peanuts (or other nuts) finely chopped.

Method: Cream cheese with sugar, peanut butter and vanilla essence. Add more sugar if needed to give a manageable paste.

Roll the mixture into 10 balls and roll each one in chopped nuts to coat completely. Place in sweet paper.

Makes 10 sweets.

Peppermint Mice

450g/1 lb sieved icing sugar
3 tablespoons liquid glucose
1 lightly whisked egg white
A few drops of peppermint essence

Decoration:
24 currants - eyes
12 coloured balls - nose
24 pieces angelica - whiskers
24 flaked almonds - ears
12 pieces string or liquorice - tail

Method: Place the sugar and glucose in a bowl. Add enough egg white to make a manageable paste. On a well sugared surface, divide the mixture into 12. Shape into mice.

Makes 12 mice.

Santa's Treats (need to heat some ingredients)

25g/1oz butter
2 tablespoons sieved cocoa
150ml/1/4pt sweetened condensed milk
225g/8oz crushed digestive biscuits
50g/2oz chopped glace cherries
50g/2oz hazelnuts (or other nuts that can be roasted and chopped)
Finely grated rind and juice of 1 orange
50g/2 oz desiccated coconut

Method: Place butter, cocoa and milk in a pan and heat together until melted. Add all other ingredients except coconut. With damp hands, shape the mixture into 36 balls and roll in coconut. Place the sweets in sweet papers.

Makes 36 sweets

Session 5
ALL CHANGE FOR A BLIND MAN
Mark 10:46-52

> WE WANT THE CHILDREN... to see how much Jesus cares and that He has the power to make things better.

DO

1. 'Feely Bag'

➤ Have a bag, preferably with a draw string, and put a number of everyday objects inside (for example, a small brush, a wax crayon, a coin, a flannel... different textures, but nothing sharp!)

YOU WILL NEED
To prepare the 'feely bag'

1. Have the children sit in a circle

2. Pass round the 'feely bag' (starting with a leader who sets the pattern).

3. Each person has a short time to feel one of the objects (no peeping, of course!) and then says:
   "I can feel something..... (hard, soft, small... and so on), I think it is a ....."

4. When the bag gets back to the leader, go over the suggestions and then open up the bag to see who was right - this is the exciting bit, so build up the suspense!

2. Guess the smell!

➤ Find a number of things which have a distinctive smell (for example, coffee, orange, onion, soap, crisps, cheese...)

YOU WILL NEED
To collect things with a strong smell
A blindfold

YOU MAY NEED
A small prize

1. Ask for two or three volunteers.

2. Blindfold one of the volunteers, and ask the others to wait outside with another leader.

3. Pass each thing under the nose of the blindfolded volunteer and ask him/her to guess what it is just by smelling it.

4. Have the other children applaud and cheer any correct answer!

5. Continue with each of the volunteers - award a prize to the child who guesses most correctly if you wish.

2.   Obstacle Course

1. Ask for three volunteers, and blindfold them.

2. Set out a simple obstacle course, like the one below:

a cushion	- to avoid
a box	- to step over
a chair	- to sit on
a mug of water	- to pick up and drink

   As you are putting out the obstacles, explain to the volunteers what they have to do at each obstacle.

3. Ask the children to do the course as follows:

   Volunteer 1 -   completely on his/her own!

   Volunteer 2 -   on his/her own, with the other children shouting 'helpful' instructions

   Volunteer 3 -   with a leader holding his/her hand and guiding him/her through it

4. If you want to develop this into a team game, shift and swap the obstacles between each round.

YOU WILL NEED
A series of simple obstacles
Blindfolds

HEAR

Set the Scene...

★ Talk briefly about the games, stressing how difficult it was not to be able to see. If you do the obstacle course, bring out how much easier it was with help.

Tell the story twice -

THE FIRST TIME, simply read it, using the following outline:

Story

Imagine what it would be like if you couldn't see! If you couldn't see anything; not even a flower, your breakfast, a friend's face or even your own toes!

Bartimaeus was like that. He couldn't see a thing. Every day his friends would lead him down to the village, sit him down at the edge of the road and leave him there. He would shout out to passers-by and ask them for money. The sun beat down and the roads were hot and dusty. There were no cars or buses or bicycles but lots of people with donkeys and camels, who stirred up the dirt and dust. For Bartimaeus, the days seemed long and tiring.

Then one day, Bartimaeus heard someone say that Jesus was coming. Jesus! He had heard about Him - heard that He could make lame people walk and blind people see. Bartimaeus decided that he would listen carefully (and he was very good at listening) and when he heard the crowd coming he would shout out to Jesus.

So he waited very patiently. The hours seemed to drag by, but then he heard voices coming nearer!

"Jesus, Jesus take pity on me". Some of the crowd didn't like it:

"Shh", they said, "Be quiet!" Bartimaeus took no notice and continued to call out:

"Jesus, Jesus, help me!"
Suddenly the crowd stopped and a quiet voice said:
"Bring him to me". Some people said to Bartimaeus:
"Cheer up! Get up! He is calling you!" Bartimaeus scrambled to his feet, threw off his cloak and walked towards Jesus' voice.

"What do you want me to do for you?" said Jesus.
"I would like to be able to see"
"Go on your way" said Jesus, "you will be able to see, because you have believed in me".
Bartimaeus stared and stared and gradually he realised that he could see shapes instead of blackness. The shapes formed themselves into a smiling face.

"I can see! I can see!" Bartimaeus shouted and he danced up and down with joy.

THE SECOND TIME, involve the children with 'rhythmic speaking'.

➡ Choose individual children (or leaders) to play JESUS and BARTIMAEUS, and divide the rest of the group in half: Group 1 and Group 2.

You may wish to do this more than once, to allow different children to take the main roles! You can vary the beats and rhythms, but here is a script to start with: just say the lines and the children will soon catch on!

Leader	**Blind Bartimaeus was sitting by the road side**
Group 1	**Blind Bar-ti-ma-eus, blind Bar-ti-ma-eus**
Group 2	**Could not see a thing, could not see a thing**

Repeat last two lines several times (they can also be said together as the rhythm fits) until Bartimaeus breaks in with...

Bartimaeus	**Je-sus will heal me, Je-sus will heal me**
Group 1	**Shout His name, shout His name**
Group 2	**Sh-sh-sh. Don't make a fuss**

These lines can also be repeated and said together

These lines can also be repeated and said together

Bartimaeus   **Je-sus will heal me, Je-sus will heal me**
              Je-sus, Je-sus, Je-sus!

The next part is spoken normally:

Jesus   **What do you want me to do?**

Bartimaeus   **I would like to be able to see**

Bartimaeus   **I can see! I can see! I can see!**
              Wheee....... (sound getting louder!)

Everybody   **(cheers very loudly in any way they like!)**

SING

The first five verses of the 'All Change!' theme song

SEE

➤ Colour the figure of Bartimaeus.

➥ Tack it over the fifth part of the frieze

TALK, THINK AND PRAY

☆ Ask: *What did Jesus do for Bartimaeus?*

☆ Bring out especially how much Jesus cares and that He has the special powers to make people better, - without tablets, or medicines or hospital operations!

☆ Mention that Jesus made many people well again - people who could not walk, people who had skin diseases - and even people who had died.

☆ Go on to say that God has given us doctors and nurses today to help sick people get better, but that we can still ask Jesus to help!

☆ Ask the children about anybody they know who is ill, and write each name down.

☆ **PRAY**

... thanking God for our sight
... thanking God for doctors and nurses (and other health workers your children might be involved with)
... asking Jesus to help each individual mentioned by the children
... thanking Jesus that He cares and has the power to heal.

◄ **YOU WILL NEED**
To prepare the figure in advance
The frieze
Glue or blu-tack

DO

YOU WLL NEED
To make a braille verse and photocopies of page 42 (enough for one per child)
A large piece of paper
Pens or pencils

1. Braille Verse

In advance, make one large copy of the braille verse on page 42. Mark out the correct pattern of dots softly with a pencil on a large sheet of paper. Now work your way through, press anything small and round (a seed or a pip would work well!) carefully into the back of the paper, this will raise the dot so that it can be felt!

1. Explain (briefly) what braille is, and how blind people using their sense of touch can read.

2. Show your braille verse - let the children shut their eyes and carefully feel the raised dots.

3. Now give out the individual copies, and ask the children to break the code and find out what the message says!

4. Children who finish quickly or who enjoy this could be asked to write their own name or another message in braille!

YOU WILL NEED
A large piece of coloured paper
Coloured pens, paints or crayons
OR Magazines
Scissors
Glue

2. Collage

Encourage the children **EITHER** to draw and paint pictures of things they would really miss looking at (for example, somebody's face, the TV, a pet dog... and so on) **OR** to cut exciting and attractive pictures out of magazines. Stick them to the paper, adding the words:

THANK YOU LORD, THAT WE CAN SEE.

YOU WILL NEED
A tape recorder
A plain cassette tape
A separate room

3. Tape the Story

Building on the theme of using senses other than sight, have groups of children record their version of the Bartimaeus story on to tape: this would best be done group by group, whilst the other children are busy with something else! Play the tape to everyone at the end of the session - they will enjoy listening to their own voices!

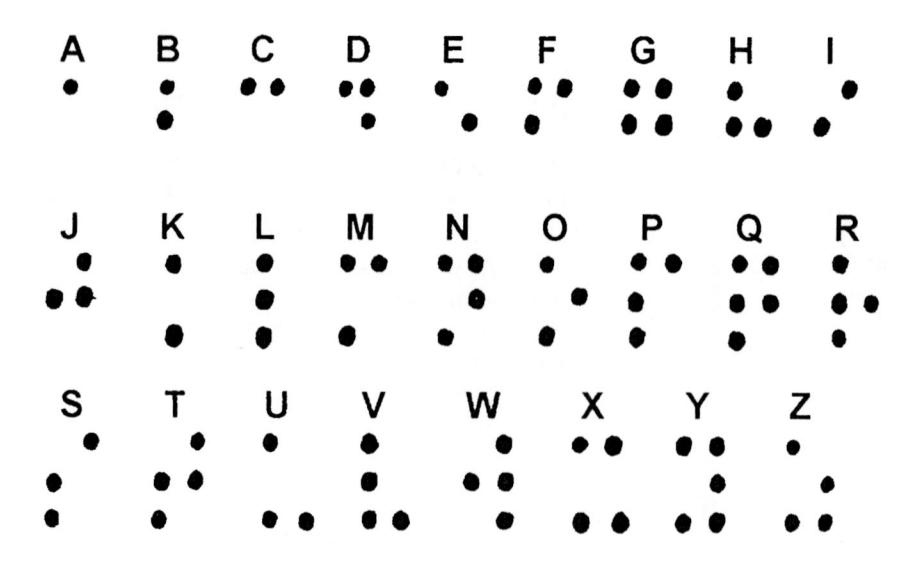

A	B	C	D	E	F	G	H	I
J	K	L	M	N	O	P	Q	R
S	T	U	V	W	X	Y	Z	

Blind people use their fingers to read. By feeling a pattern of dots they can read books, newspapers and letters. This is called BRAILLE. Can you use the BRAILLE alphabet to understand this message from the Bible?

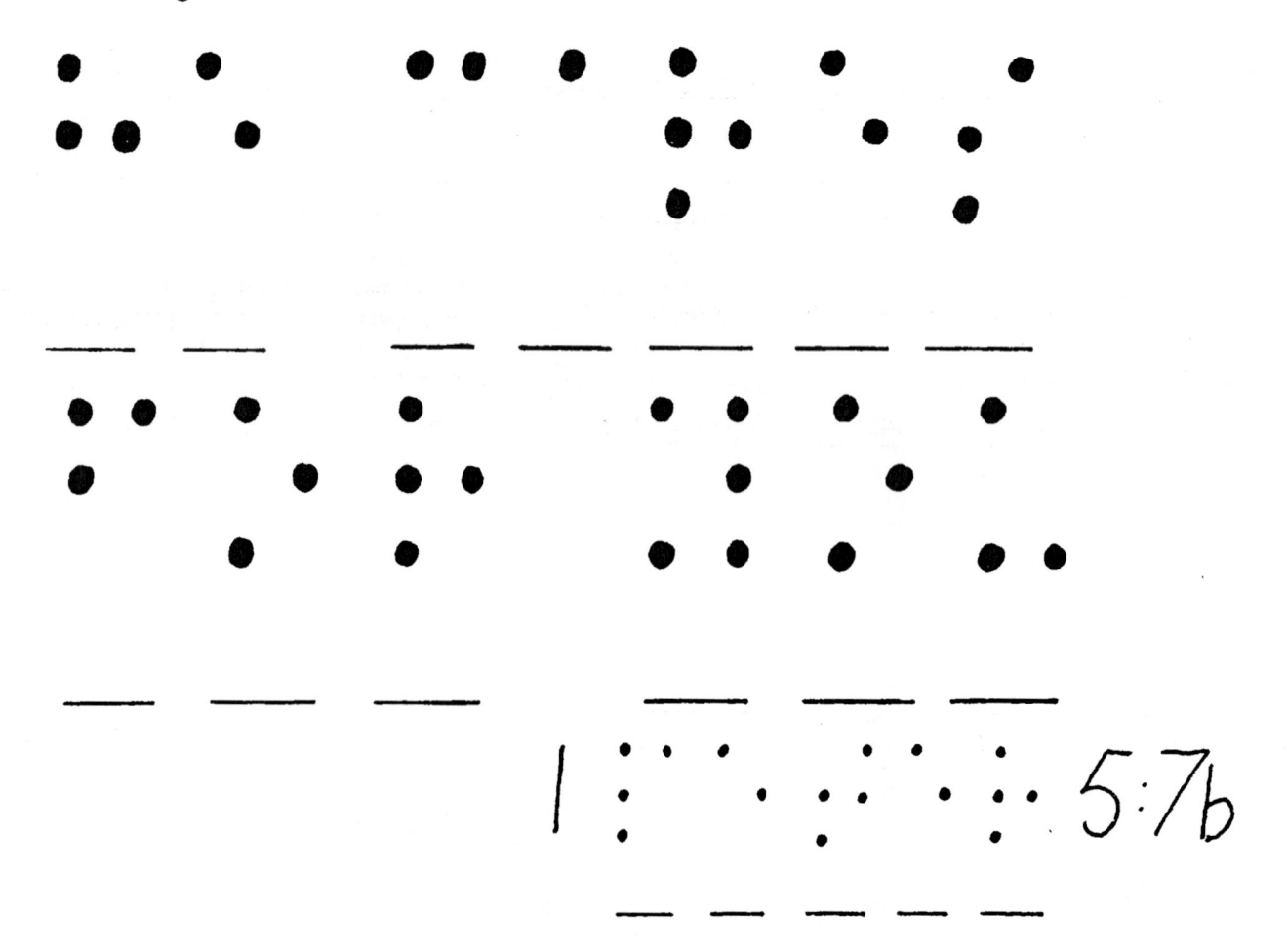

_ _ _ _ _ _ _

_ _ _ _ _ _ _ 1: _ _ _ _ _ _ 5:7b
_ _ _ _ _

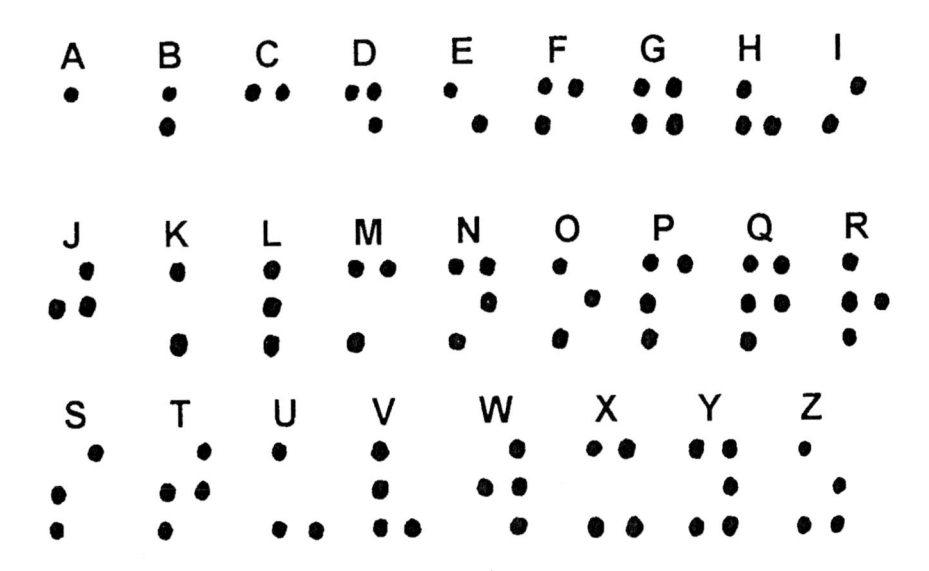

A	B	C	D	E	F	G	H	I

J	K	L	M	N	O	P	Q	R

S	T	U	V	W	X	Y	Z

Blind people use their fingers to read. By feeling a pattern of dots they can read books, newspapers and letters. This is called BRAILLE. Can you use the BRAILLE alphabet to understand this message from the Bible?

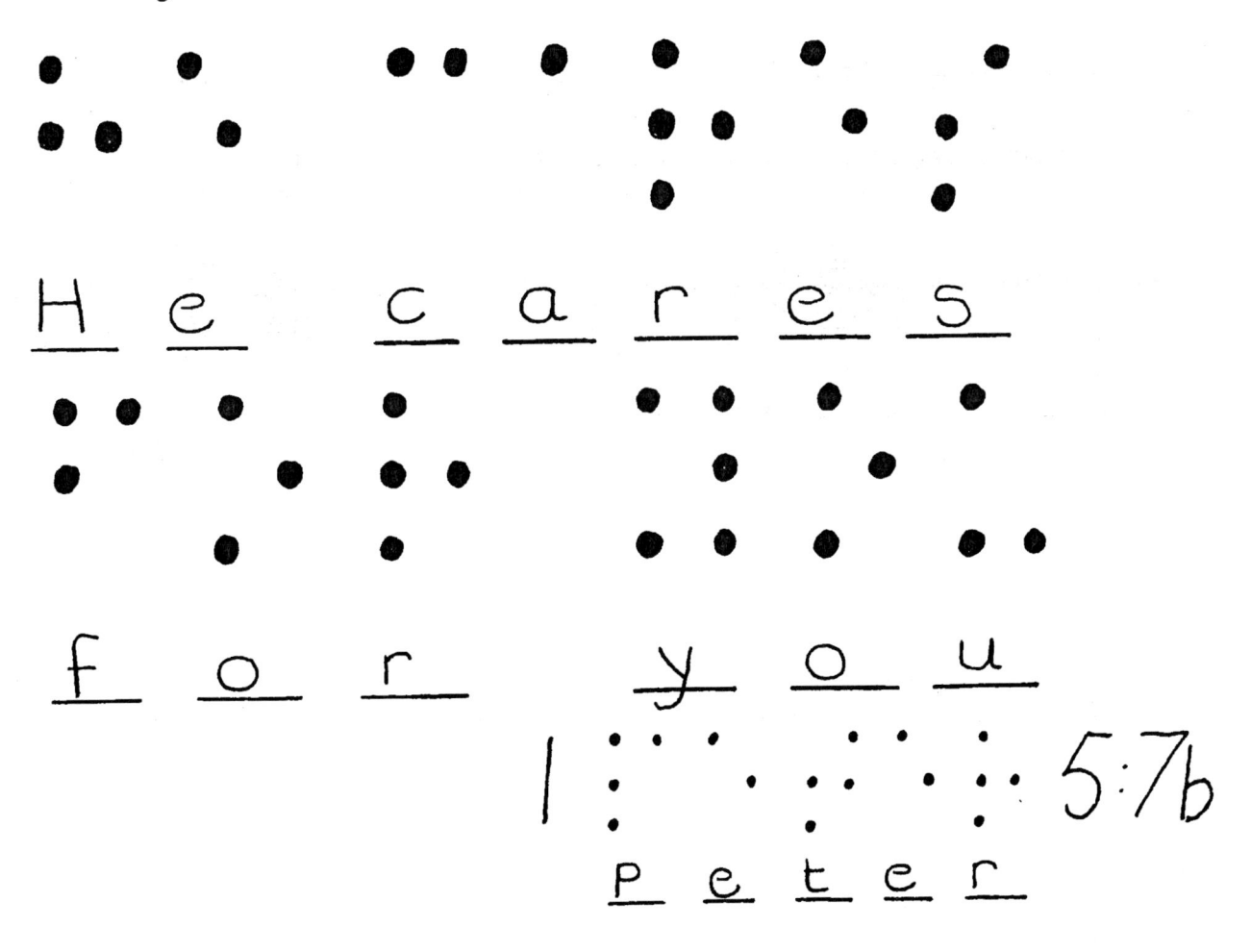

He cares

for you

1 Peter 5:7b

Session 6
ALL CHANGE FOR A HUNGRY CROWD
Mark 6:30-44

> WE WANT THE CHILDREN... to understand that Jesus can turn something small and ordinary given to Him into something much greater!

DO

1. 'Fish' Sandwiches

➤ You may wish to prepare part of this activity in advance, for example, by getting the bread and butter ready before the session.

1. Spread the bread with butter and add the fish paste - NB It is best to spread this very thinly in case the children do not like the flavour!

2. Let the children use the cutter to press out fish-shaped sandwiches **OR** just cut the sandwiches into small fingers or triangles.

3. <u>Save</u> the sandwiches until after the story...

2. Flapping the Fish

➤ In advance, copy, cut out (and colour, if you wish) the fish outline and the bread outline on page 50.
Roll up and sellotape together 3 or 4 sheets of newspaper.

1. Divide the children into two equal teams - 'the fish' and 'the bread'.

2. Give the first child in each team the rolled-up newspaper and either the fish or the bread outline.

3. On the word 'go', the fish or bread outlines are put on the floor and the newspaper is waved hard behind it to create a draught of air!

4. When the fish or bread has been moved the length of the room, the child picks it up and runs back to his or her team - the next child takes over, and the race continues until everybody has had a turn.

5. The team to finish first has won!

YOU MAY NEED ➤
To prepare in advance

YOU WILL NEED
Sliced bread
Butter or margarine
Fish paste
A spreading knife
If possible, a fish-shaped cutter

YOU WILL NEED ➤
To prepare the fish/bread outlines and make the 'flapper'

YOU MAY NEED
Small prizes for the winning team

HEAR

Set the Scene...

★ Talk about picnics, along the following guidelines:

- *Have you ever been on a picnic?*
- *Where did you go?*
- *What did you have to eat?*

Establish that the most important thing to have on a picnic is FOOD! Go on to say that today's Bible story is about the biggest picnic ever... but there was no food!

▶ **Tell the story -**

Story

◀ **YOU WILL NEED**
To make copies of the pictures on pages 51-56

Lots and lots of people followed Jesus because of all the special things He said and did...

★ Ask: **Can you remember any of those things?** and bring out particularly any of the stories from the last five sessions.

One day, many people had come out on to a hillside to listen to Jesus - it was a huge crowd...

➡ Show picture 1

➡ The Bible says '5,000 men, not counting the women and children' - try to give the children some idea of the size of the crowd; for example, it's about ten primary schools.

Jesus had been talking with the people and making people better, and nobody really noticed that the hours were ticking by. When the evening came and the sun went down, people started to feel very hungry and their tummies began to rumble.
  "It's very late" said one of Jesus' friends, "let's send the crowd away to get some food"
  "No", said Jesus, "you give them something to eat".
  "But Jesus", said Philip, "it would cost lots of money to buy enough food for this many people!".
  "Go and see how much food you have got" said Jesus.
Now one little boy had brought a picnic lunch - there were only five little bread rolls and two fish, but he decided to show it to one of Jesus' friends called Andrew. Andrew took it to Jesus.
  "There's a boy here with his picnic, five bread rolls and two fish - but that won't be enough for all these people!" he said. Jesus just told his friends to ask the crowds of people to sit down. Jesus took the five bread rolls and the two fish and said 'thank you' to God for the food. Then He asked His friends to start to give the food out... now there were not only five little bread rolls and two fish, but plenty of food for every single

➡ Show picture 2

➡ Show picture 3

➡ Show picture 4

➡ Show picture 5

→ Show picture 6

person in the huge crowd! And there was even some left over at the end!

→ Hand out the fish sandwiches you made at the beginning - and eat them together!

SING

The 'All Change!' theme song!

SEE

YOU WILL NEED
To prepare the picture
The frieze
Blu-tack or glue

➤ In advance, copy and colour the final part of the frieze.

→ Tack it over the empty plates.

TALK, THINK AND PRAY

→ To reinforce the story:
- jumble round the pictures, and ask the children to put them in the right order - **what happened first..? and then..?** and so on;

- now see if the children can tell you the story - show the pictures one by one, and encourage them to say what is happening in each.

★ Focus the children's attention on the boy, emphasising that:

- he was just like any of the children in your group

- he could have chosen to keep his lunch for himself

- he thought he only had something very ordinary to offer Jesus

★ Ask the children: **What happened to the bread and the fish?**

★ Bring out clearly that only Jesus could do this, because He was so special and had God's powers.

★ Say that Jesus still uses ordinary people who choose to give Him ordinary things.

★ Mention a few examples, such as:

- 1p doesn't seem much, but if we all choose to save 1p's they can be used to help people in need.

- ★ Five minutes spent talking to someone doesn't seem much, but if we choose to do this, perhaps to an old person, we can really cheer them up and make their day!

- ★ Ask the children for other suggestions.

  [Ultimately, of course, Jesus asks us to give up everything, to follow Him - you may or may not feel that it is appropriate to develop this idea at this stage.]

★ Extend the 'discussion' if you can, relating it to your particular group:

- some children don't feel that they are good at things and that they have anything at all to offer

- some groups might like to think of a particular project to work towards - eg collecting money for a specific cause.

- some children may feel ready to make a choice for Jesus.

★ **PRAY**

★ State that Jesus can use our prayers too!

1. Divide the children into 3 groups, preferably with a leader in each.

2. Ask each group to think of (and to write down, if you wish) their own prayers.

   Group 1 -   'thank you' prayers
   Group 2 -   'sorry' prayers
   Group 3 -   'please' prayers

3. Have a prayer time led by children from each group.

YOU MAY NEED
Pencils
Paper

DO

1. Fish Mobiles
➤ In advance, cut strips of paper or thin card - you will need a good number of 30 cm x 3 cm strips (eg A4 divided into 7 lengthways) and also double the number of shorter strips 10 cm x 3 cm.

➡ Make up the mobiles, following the instructions on page 57.

2. Fish Search
➤ In advance, cut out 11 fish shapes, perhaps using copies of the outline on page 50 once more. On each fish shape, write separate words (and then the reference) from the following verse:

| THE | CROWDS | WERE | ALL | AMAZED | AT |

| WHAT | JESUS | HAD | DONE | MATTHEW 12:23 |

◀ **YOU WILL NEED**
To cut strips of different coloured paper
Wool
A stapler
Glue
Wire coathangers
OR
Lengths of dowling
◀ **YOU WILL NEED**
To prepare the fish outlines

Hide the fish around the room before the session - some in obvious places, but make some not so obvious!

➡ 1. Ask the children to search for the fish you have hidden.

2. When a child finds a fish, he/she should bring it back to the leader.

3. When all the fish have been found, gather the children together and look at all the words - can the children put them in the right order to make a sentence from the Bible? Provide help and hints according to the needs of your group.

★ You may wish to comment briefly on the verse.

3. Fish Badges

YOU WILL NEED
Pieces of stiff card about 6cm x 6cm
Sellotape
Safety pins
Coloured pens, pencils or crayons

★ Say that Jesus' friends and followers had a special code, like a 'password' and explain that this was a fish shape!

★ Mention that people today sometimes have a fish sign to show that they are following Jesus.

Have the children make fish badges:

1. Give a piece of card to each child and ask them to draw and colour a fish on it.

2. Sellotape a safety pin to the back of the fish...

➡ Encourage the children to wear the badges now (and at home and school!) to show that they want to be Jesus' friends too!

FISH AND BREAD OUTLINES

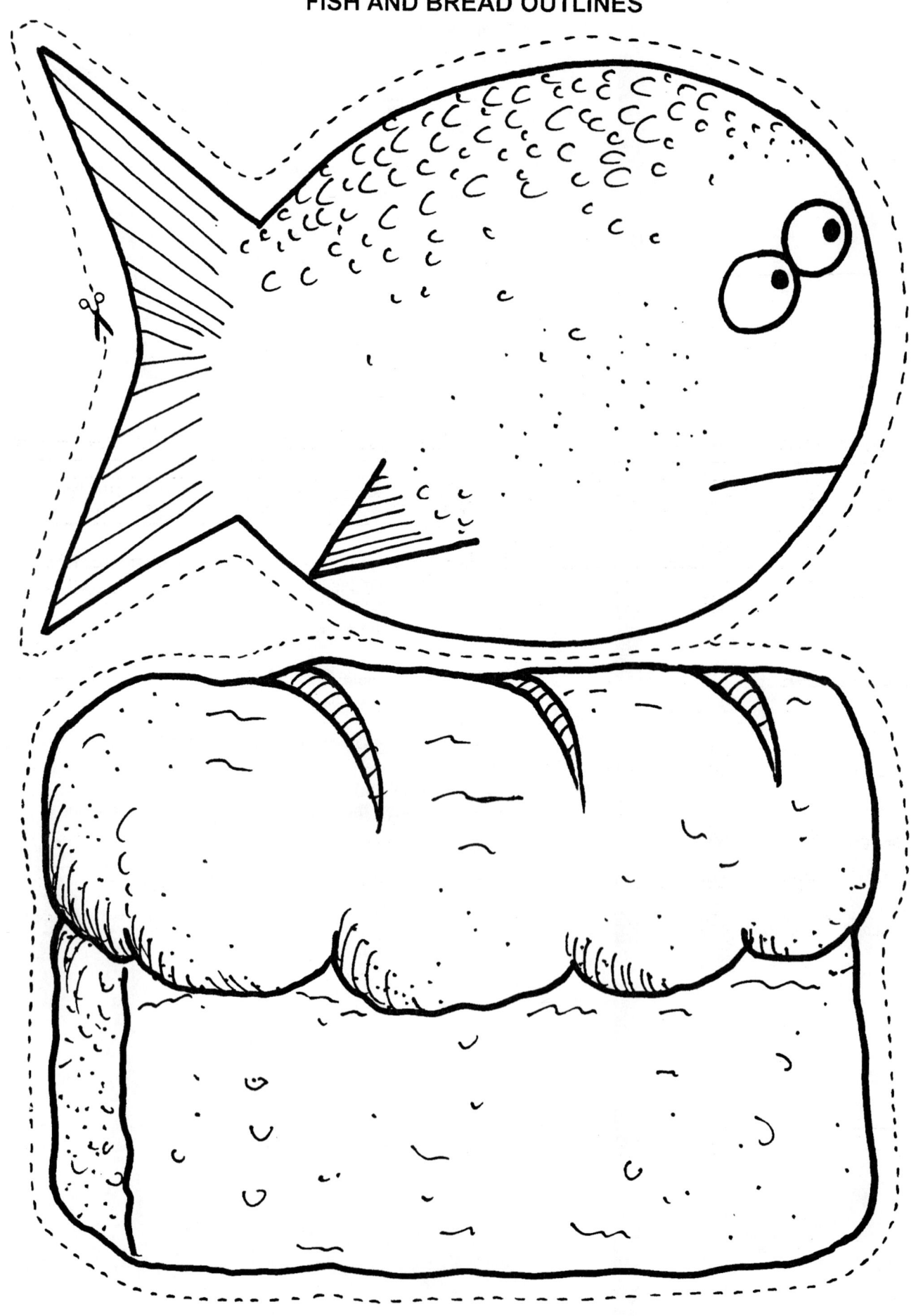

Picture 1

Picture 2

Picture 3

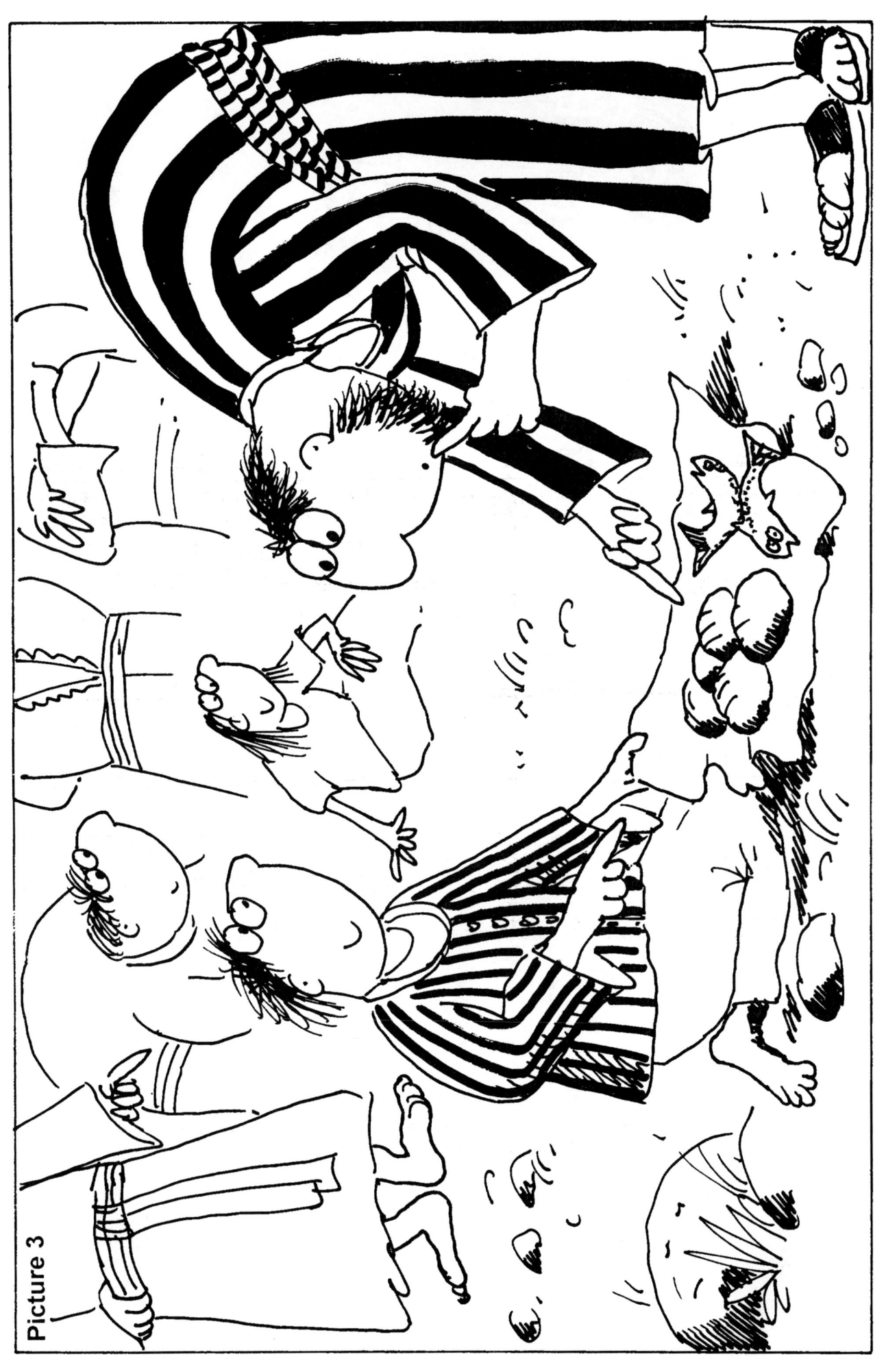

Picture 4

Picture 5

Picture 6

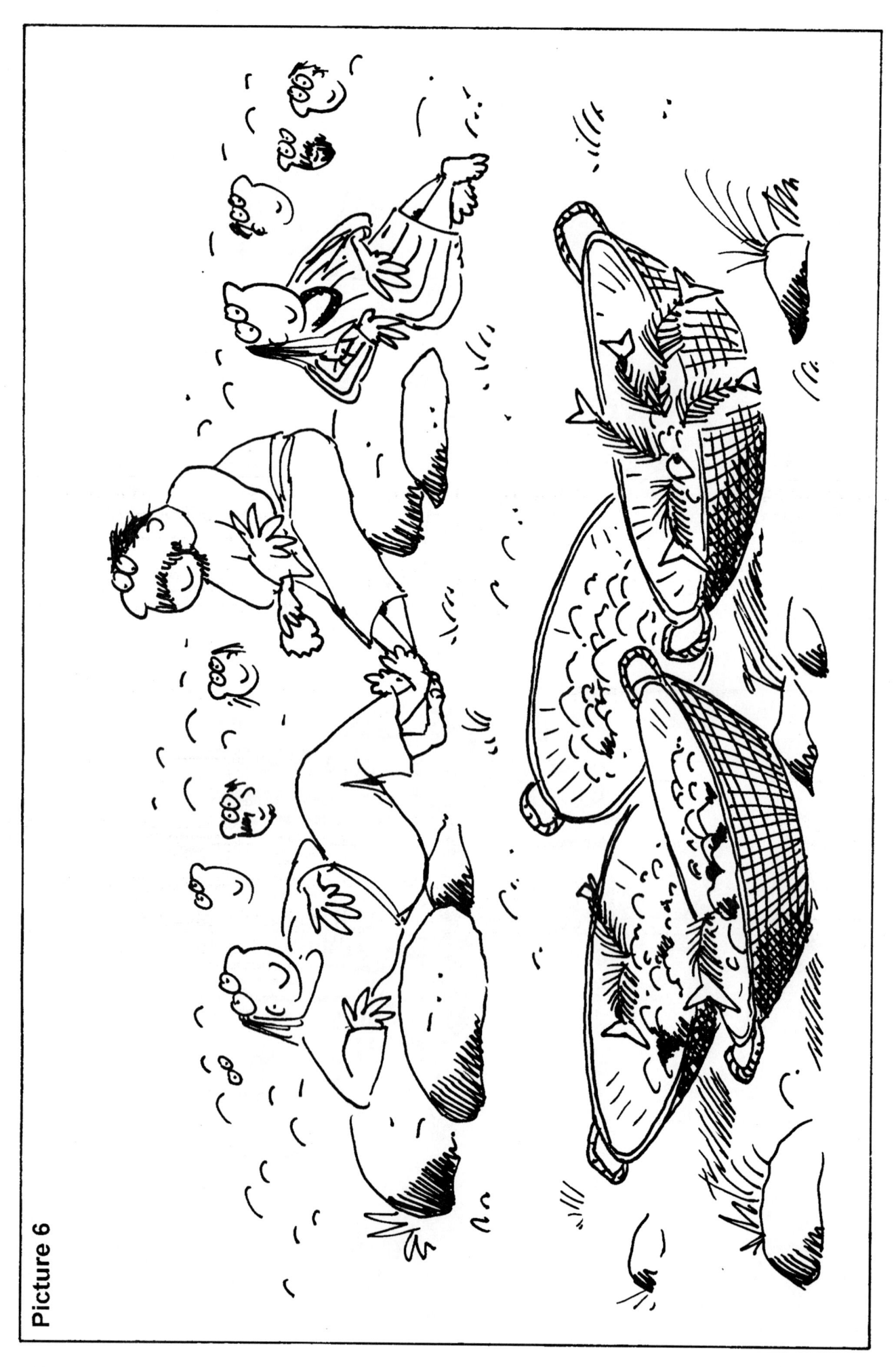

HOW TO MAKE A FISH MOBILE

For materials see page 53.

1. Take a long strip of paper and fold it gently in half - staple it about 5 cm in to form the tail.

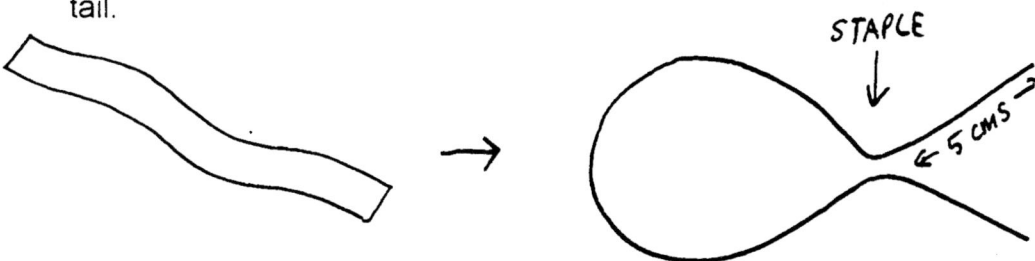

2. Now take two short strips of paper - fold them in half, and then fold back from each edge to form a flap.

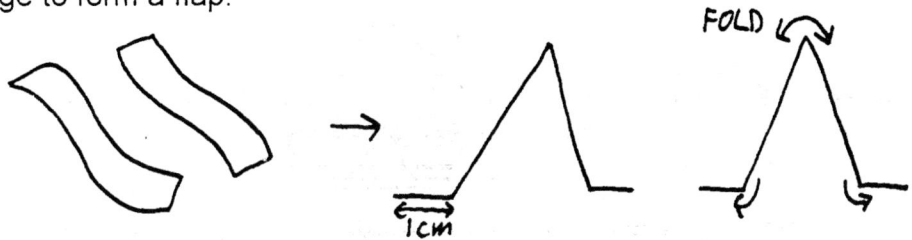

3. Glue the flaps and stick them to the fish to make fins.

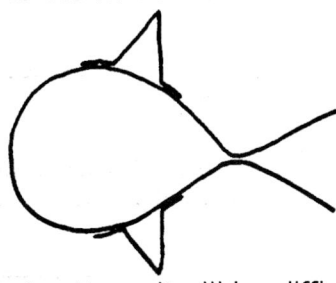

4. Attach a length of fine wool (not cotton - it will be difficult to see when it gets tangled!) to each fish.

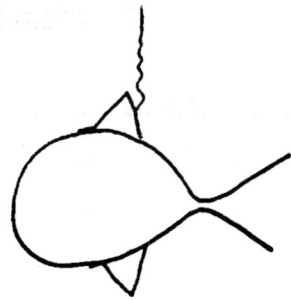

5. Use the fish on their own, or hang several different coloured ones from a wire coathanger or length of dowling to make a mobile.

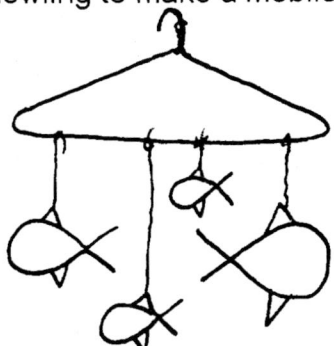

'ALL CHANGE!'

'All Change!'

Verse 1
: Jesus went to a wedding at Cana
Where the people had run out of wine.
He said: "Fill up these stone jars with water"
Then Jesus changed it into finest wine!

Chorus:
: All Change, all change!
Come see what Jesus can do
All change, all change!
King Jesus makes everything new.

Verse 2
: Jesus called to His friends who were fishing
Simon, Andrew and James and John
"Leave your nets for a new kind of fishing
I've a brand new way for you to walk along".

Verse 3
: Jesus slept as a big storm was breaking
and his friends were afraid they'd all drown
When they woke Him He said "Don't you trust me?"
At His Word the storm died down and all was calm.

Verse 4
: Jesus called to a man named Zacchaeus
"I must stay at your house today"
Bad Zacchaeus had been cheating and greedy
But he changed and said "I'll follow in Your way".

Verse 5
: Jesus saw Bartimaeus the beggar
Who was blind and was longing to see
"Lord please take away my blindness!"
Jesus said "You are made well through trusting me"

Verse 6
: It was late and the crowd were all hungry
Jesus said "Give them something to eat"
Though His friends had so little to offer,
Jesus took it and He made a great big feast!

Penny Bainbridge © 1993

'ALL CHANGE!'

Verse 1
Jesus went to a wedding at Cana
Where the people had run out of wine.
He said: "Fill up these stone jars with water"
Then Jesus changed it into finest wine!

Chorus:
All Change, all change!
Come see what Jesus can do
All change, all change!
King Jesus makes everything new.

Verse 2
Jesus called to His friends who were fishing
Simon, Andrew and James and John
"Leave your nets for a new kind of fishing
I've a brand new way for you to walk along".

Verse 3
Jesus slept as a big storm was breaking
and his friends were afraid they'd all drown
When they woke Him He said "Don't you trust me?"
At His Word the storm died down and all was calm.

Verse 4
Jesus called to a man named Zacchaeus
"I must stay at your house today"
Bad Zacchaeus had been cheating and greedy
But he changed and said "I'll follow in Your way".

Verse 5
Jesus saw Bartimaeus the beggar
Who was blind and was longing to see
"Lord please take away my blindness!"
Jesus said "You are made well through trusting me"

Verse 6
It was late and the crowd were all hungry
Jesus said "Give them something to eat"
Though His friends had so little to offer,
Jesus took it and He made a great big feast!

Penny Bainbridge © 1993